M000013878

BIG SILENCES
IN A
YEAR OF RAIN

DORIS FERLEGER

MAIN STREET RAG PUBLISHING COMPANY
CHARLOTTE, NORTH CAROLINA

Cover photograph by Joan Webb
Cover design by Susan Deikman and M. Scott Douglass
Photograph of author by Jeff Mantler

ACKNOWLEDGMENTS

Grateful acknowledgment is made to the editors of the following publications in which these poems first appeared, sometimes in earlier versions:

Calyx: "Flooding and Floating"
Comstock Review: "Spell to Be Said upon Hearing the Pain of a Loved One" (Muriel Craft Bailey finalist), "Dark Horse"
Jewish Currents: "Beaches before Me"
Northeast Corridor: "His Breath in My Hands"
Lullwater: "Readying"
Phoebe: Journal of Gender and Cultural Critiques: "Praying to a Stone" (published as "Praying at Your Bedside")
South Carolina Review: "Flooding and Floating"

Library of Congress Control Number: 2010933615

ISBN 13: 978-1-59948-258-3

Produced in the United States of America

Main Street Rag
PO Box 690100
Charlotte, NC 28227
www.MainStreetRag.com

CONTENTS

Part 3: *Fit-for-Life*

Part 4: *Touch Falling*

PROLOGUE: READYING

READYING

To ready myself for love
I must dispose of the dead
bodies I have romanced, rubbing against
their rough cloth. I must remove
 all my white wedding clothes
and black, especially black clothes, raiments
of the fathers and the fathers' fathers, remove
my long beard of hope, remove my gold
rings carved with initials that once belonged

to a stranger, remove my long list of family names
on the roll calls in the newly available archives
of Majdanek, Theresienstadt, Bergen-Belsen
my brother is still finding, rounding up,
all those names filling pages. He finds also
two paintings by Dürer of a woman who bears
our last name. In one, her long waves of hair are ready
for love. In the other her hair is pushed
tight against her face.

See the photo of the eighth sister,
her husband was the only one who made a living,
I am told, the one with a dry goods store, see how
she shows puffs of silk for sleeves, poses
with her left shoulder facing
the camera. Her eyes are very large and full
of sadness and something
other than love.

I am readying myself for love
which means I am trying to leave
my history behind. You see, I have been calling

on the dead to come down and play the way
my mother called on them alive, especially
her niece who, like my mother, had been
a hopeful girl in Warsaw Ghetto's pungent streets.

My mother told me once and only once
of the young man in the Ghetto, a boy really,
when she was hungry, how he played
with her hair, her fingers, how he played them too,
like harmonica and hope. A dark hope
that nothing lasting would come of it, would come
from all that hunger and those young stirring seconds.

What did they do for love?
Psychologists say it's better to tell the children
what happened, better than having them guess.
I don't know. Still I guess at what they did for love.
I am readying myself for love, getting naked,
but less naked than I must become in order to enter
the mikvah baths, where the rough, or is she kind,
woman holds out two rough, or are they soft,
bleached towels and makes sure I have
nothing, am holding back nothing, am ready
to drown or stand straight in the stream of life.

No blood stains must linger, no odors
of the dead must still cling.
Before the plunge I must cut my
fingernails, place the clippings in a little pile
and flush them away as it is written,
one must not leave even one of their dead
nails lying unburied on the ground.

Doris Ferleger

Finally I must give up hope
that their nails are not scattered about
like tombstones stolen from Jewish graves
to pave roads and sidewalks in the Old Country
on which steps are still being taken.

*

What keeps me from love?
What keeps me from singing hallelujahs
every time your fingers stroll and skip
on my streets, my sidewalks?

PART 1: CAN YOU SEE MY EYES?

CAN YOU SEE MY EYES?

If you run away to the circus
I will be the tight rope. If you run
away to the sea I will be the sail,
I read to my son from *The Run Away Bunny.*
I used to wonder if any other mother found
the book disturbing—the mother
bunny traveling the world after her boy
so he can't even run away. I used to dream
I was still living in my childhood house,
even years after I had moved out,
gotten married, left with my husband
to live in another country, gotten very sick
for long years bargaining with the old
God of my childhood, *If you make me*
*better I promise I will…*While I waited
for God to keep His promise I held
a warm wash cloth, threadbare
against my face. *God, this is my face,*
my bare face under my rent veil.
Can you see my eyes? Are they like
the eyes of a changeling or the stranger
who stood so many years ago, legs stretched
wide apart on the small square of lawn
in front of our old row house, his face
turned upward to sky, mouth
open like the moon
breathing in the not yet night-
shift air, breathing out his boozy breath?
God, how he sang as though the poor earth
he stood on had entered his feet and turned
to lava somewhere deeper inside of him
than anyone had ever been.

Momma averted her eyes
and pulled all of us around
to the back alley, through
our basement door, the one
we never used before
or after. The Elvis-looking boy
next door, who lifted
the laundry pole for strength
training, had dropped
the clothes pins on our driveway
in a heap that looked like so many
clowns' earrings. Hearing the drunkard
still singing on our lawn out front,
the trolley cars trundling by,
the cockroaches scampering
in and out of the drain, Momma put up
the tea kettle until it, too,
couldn't stop singing.

Doris Ferleger

INVISIBLE

Two long brooms, momma calls my blue-black
hair she brushes into a wide fan across my bed,

sets in pink sponge rollers that look like they
can't hurt to sleep on, but do. The big dumb dog

beside me is no comfort. I don't really like him at all,
never hold him, never even bothered to name him,

but because my father bought him for me,
I let him sleep, pink and floppy, stuffed

between my bed and wall, though for years
he has disturbed my sense of aloneness.

I can't forget the dog came from Ozzy's store,
Ozzy our neighbor with a cross-

bite who still calls us *the refs*.
Momma sets our hair the same, waves everywhere

and one big dipper clipped on our wide foreheads
with a fake rhinestone bobby. Momma looks

lovely though invisible, sitting on the other side
of poppa in *shul*. Anyone who can't follow

poppa's pointing finger as it rolls under each Hebrew word
is invisible to me. Momma's good for cherry lozenges

she keeps in her forbidden purse. *Manyele, you'll count ceiling
beams in shul when you're a married one. Sit! Study! The rabbi comes!*

Bubba Hinde Leah had warned, but momma had
more important things to do at fourteen, running

the ruddy children raw in Warsaw's snowfalls,
turning the three room house into a school in daylight,

bedding rolled up to make it look like a carefree
classroom for the kids whose parents still had

a little money before Warsaw turned dark.
Momma isn't impressed with the men who line

the altar, all in holy-white from *kittels* to Keds.
Kittels—muslin robes that will some day be their shrouds.

Keds— canvas since anything made from the dead is
forbidden in *shul* on this holiest of holies.

Shul is no place for Momma to love. How she washed
her father's stony feet back in the Old County,

his illness even leeches couldn't suck out, how she
would turn poppa over and over in his sore bed

of unforgiving years, how she would twist
her cheeks and say, *Oy a broch, just like mine tatta,*

he lays—how only in washing, watching, worrying
did momma come to God—did God come to momma.

As if lifting a gleeful, drooling baby, each man hoists
a Torah over his head while singing of praise and

destruction in equal parts. On each white satin garment
that dresses each Torah, my father fashioned two lions

Doris Ferleger

that rise up on their haunches, face each other and bare
their uneven fangs, unruly manes, ready for a kill.

Each other or a common enemy? I never asked
what poppa meant when he made those lions roar,

embroidered their murderous teeth, their wilderness.
In *shul* I turn my back on momma, make her

disappear so I can be poppa's child, just
the two of us belonging to the tribe of the sacred text;

Hebrew letters undulate like meaty belly-dancers,
swell and shimmy against fine-skinned pages,

ankle-bells jingle out of our mouths. The smell of must.
My father moves his dark index finger under

each word as if the text is a map to his Old Country,
so I am never lost, though he keeps one place

all for himself, to get lost in or to locate *the disappeared*.
Like momma, I am forbidden from the *bimah*,

but I don't care as long as I get to stay inside
my father's country, his wilderness, where

the only way to love is with dismay, guilt,
unfathomable mourning of people frozen in time,

perfect victims given no time to do anything
fortunate or unforgivable.

JACKFRUIT

is the same as guava
it says so on the bottle of
Super-vitamin water I drink
for the sweetness that reminds me of
red plums Tanta Hoyna always carried
in plastic bags to the beach, and peaches
all fuzzy and dripping with bright yellow
juice, cheap bushel baskets full
bought at roadside stands on the way
to the Jersey shore. In bad times
Tanta Hoyna would pun
in her Hungarian accent,
Dis is vat you girls call
da pits, yes? Then she'd hold up
the plastic bag full of the empty fruit
seeds stripped dry of any
sweetness. My uncle Henek,
who we suspected might have taken
revenge with his big bare hands
on a Nazi, would bring home
syrups—amber, red,
turquoise—such dazzling
sweetness we'd pour over our crushed
ice and suck our hearts out.

Doris Ferleger

BEACHES BEFORE ME

In childhood my mother laid beaches before me,
Jersey beaches, Atlantic City in the 1950's. Sand, silk
and warm, peaches sweet and wet. Blue paper napkins

caught the juicy drips. Between 1943 and 1945
my mother cleaned Nazi toilets for her life; in Majdanek,
dead bodies lay before her like striped stones;

she stepped over them like nothing, dreaming her legs
to move. On the fine sand at Dover Avenue beach
my mother proudly unpacked the bright yellow

shovel and blue bucket, slid open the green and white
striped umbrella and adjusted the bobby pins in her
shoulder-length permed hair. She looked like

all the other mothers except for the dark blue
number tattooed on her left forearm. We dug deep
down to where the sand gets cool and grey and hard.

A lanky boy joined us until he spotted the tattoo:
Hey lady, were you in prison?
No. Sometimes I just forget my telephone number.

To save herself or the boy from considering
Auschwitz while the sun shone so beneficently,
she told a lie that made her sound stupid.

That night she covered Auschwitz over with a Band-Aid.
My mother talked about war in
disconnected sentences:

Sometimes I got an apple for cleaning the toilets.
A big woman there liked me.
I was always hungry.

'Go stand in the death line; today it's the life line.'
Our father was already taken.
The Belgian girls were so beautiful.

At Dover Avenue Beach I listened and watched
for one of the men in white long pants and white
button-down shirt to trudge by under the weight of his

white metal ice box, slung from a thick strap
on his sloped shoulder. *Ice cream and ices here!*
Who else? Who else?

My mother deposited one tiny silver coin into
my palm. I placed it onto the cool palm
of the sweaty man and in return he handed me

one rock-hard-ice-cream bar-covered-in-chocolate;
I held tight to the wooden stick and waited
for meltdown.

2.

At the Dover Avenue beach, my father crooned,
Oy America I love you! He loved the way waves
knocked against him, *a k-nock,* he would say,

pronouncing the *k* as in Yiddish. He'd make a fist
and swing his arm around like a windmill.
The only time my father was light

Doris Ferleger

was in the ocean. He did a sidestroke, a white film
of bubbles settling on his thin lips. Like a sea creature
shaking off its sea life, he'd shake off the water,

his trunks dripping and drooping under his pendulous belly.
A mechaya, a pleasure. Come in Miriam, though
he knew she'd never leave the shoreline.

She'd pull up his trunks and say, *De bowoch vaxed*, meaning
the belly grows fat, from eating too much after eating
too little for years in the living grave dug by the Polish

Christian couple who told the kids they were going out
to feed the pigs even though it was already dark
and they dropped raw potatoes down to where

my father lay with another Jew until Nazis stationed
for two weeks in the barn where the hole was dug
and my father could only revive the other Jew with piss.

At Dover beach, my father took pictures of me posing
at the water's edge, one leg poised in front of the other like
in ballet class, hands folded in my lap like in school.

On Dover Avenue beach my father placed his bluer
eye against the camera lens and snapped my steel
blue eyes into his own.

3.

I would like to say I remember building
sand castles with my brother, that we buried
each other's bronze bodies

with blue buckets-full of sand. But our lives were lived
as if on separate shorelines. We had lost each other
 early in an undertow of fear of losing

each other, our parents having lost
thirteen siblings between them. We had only each other,
my brother and I. To bury

each other in the fawn-colored sand
of New Jersey beaches in the 1950's—
still felt much too risky.

Doris Ferleger

VICTORY

My father used to check
if I was breathing
even when I was twelve
and thirteen. He lifted
the king-sized pillow I
hugged over my eyes. He listened
for air. I never let on
that I wasn't asleep.
My father considered
himself a success
when he found his children
still breathing. Each night
another victory
over Hitler.
I learned early
to pretend I was sleeping,
to not be a burden.

PROOF OF CITIZENSHIP

Poor-boy sweaters fit
way too tight all the way around
so they looked outgrown right
from the get-go, like the 1940's
turtle necks on news boys
who stood in the streets calling out
the latest war casualties; they cost
a whole twenty-four dollars even
in 1968 at Marianne's where
I got that credit card for free
simply by signing
my full name and smiling
all the way home, so excited
to show my father how much
I had grown, though I still shopped
with my mother and she was there
to co-sign. He said, *Let me see*,
and seemed to be examining it
for a long time, the card, that is, made of
plastic with royal-blue-block-letters
spelling my whole special name,
the first name after his murdered mother,
the middle after my mother's mother
also, by the way, sent to the ovens, though
that makes it sound like she baked
sponge cakes; there is no way
to say these things.

My father started shaking
his big round shiny head at my new
plastic sign of maturity, scrawled
with my whole sorry anglicized name
that should have been Doba Leah,

Doris Ferleger

then he chanted, *Oy, beautiful
for special skies*, and with scissors
he dissected the card before
my bug eyes, the card I coveted
as my proof of American citizenship.
I didn't dare try to take the scissors
out of his hands or even talk back.
It was a different sort of language
we spoke back then, silenced
by just a look from the father's sequined
or incendiary eyes, the Orthodox
patriarchy transported to this golden land
though the laws of keeping kosher and
resting on the Sabbath got left behind
in cinders of the shtetl.

Slicing the plastic into four unequal parts,
he said, *No kecky, no pecky, no ma'am!*
Have I already told you my father was
smitten by American sayings of all kinds?
I usually heard *this* one in our station wagon
sorties when I went along to drop off
snowsuits with fat sky blue snowmen
embroidered on the bibs for the babies
and fur coats for the moms, the silky silver
linings showed off monograms
my father had sewn with his embroidery machine.
No cash, no package, no ma'am,
he'd practice his English on me.

My classmates that year pinned
monogrammed Etienne gold
circle pins onto their heather

sweaters bought at the Villager shop.
The sweaters were also custom-
monogrammed in fancy script
just like the letters my father curly-cued
onto the linings of their mothers' furs,
in the brightly colored threads of America.

The heather sweaters had jewel-
neck-lines and hung loosely around
budded breasts, while I stuck to
the poor boy sweaters
my father paid for with cash
after the card-cutting incident,
though the sweaters made him
laugh in that needling way at
the price he paid for his daughter
to look like war's child.

It was never a question of lack
of generosity. It was just that my father
wanted me to learn to save
my own life,
to follow his lead as he took
half his weekly wage
every Friday, before the sun
went down, to the savings bank
though he always kept some cash
rolled up in his brown pair of socks
by the bed, right next to the bulky
batch of keys, just in case America
turned on us, on all our accumulated
proof of citizenship, survival, existence.

Doris Ferleger

LIVING

Deep snow and Bernie bought
his mother a spring handbag,
a fancy shmancy evening bag
in spring colors. She didn't like
the colors but she kept it as a sign

of his trust in her
living at least until
crocuses popped up.

The morning I walked over stones
in the creek, I was wearing that pale yellow
gauzy dress with tiny spring flowers tied
in bouquets all over and those girlish puffy sleeves
and a young man was playing
a harmonica
in the clover grass and it wasn't
a dream that I was alive.

ONLY SON

Imagine an only son full of promise and dark
burden peeking out from behind a makeshift

curtain that splits a one-room house in two,
at five dark-skinned beauties, sisters

primping, combing, braiding Sabbath hair,
Sabbath bread, Sabbath white; Sabbath white,

Sabbath bread, Sabbath hair. In the mirror,
he stole glimpses, searching for a reflection

of his own manhood. Imagine his father's
expectations bore down on him:

When I am old you will care for me,
help pay dowries for your sisters.

Your side locks must grow uncut.
Your top front hairs must be cut short

as the first joint of my index finger.
To make sure this was done, his father

took a scissors in the dark to the hair
growing across the sleeping son's forehead

and cut according to the laws Moses carried
down from the mountain.

You who are listening may say,
Of course. God's laws must be followed.

Or you may say how unfeeling his father was.
I say, after the cutting, the boy sneaked out

for a polka and soon left in his cousin's wagon
to find work in a distant town. You say,

It's only natural. In every generation
the shtetl grows too narrow for a young man

to breathe his bright blue breath. I say,
the year is 1934, the only son, fourteen.

In the city of Lodz he finds himself outside
a bakery, peering through glass and tears.

The owner, thinking him penniless, offers
a small cake. What the baker doesn't see is

the money-pouch sewn inside the boy's trouser-waist,
holding *zlotys* the boy is earning to send his sisters.

But the *zlotys*, saved and sent over the next
six years are not enough to save the mirror

of sisters from shattering like Jewish shop windows
on Kristallnacht, like vessels of God's light upon

the world's creation. After the shattering,
the only son of a pious Jew kept searching

inside the shards, beseeching the shards
as if they were oracles: *If I had not left?*

If I had gone with them to die?
You who are listening ask, what is at stake

for me in telling this story. I answer:
Because it is my father who leaves

it to me to remember his life through me.
Now, when that only son, who is my father,

looks at me, his only daughter, neither of us
can bear it for too long. He says: *You look*

just like my sister Ruchele—
like my sister Golde—

Mirror of sisters—
Am I his hall of mirrors?

Doris Ferleger

BROAD STREET

On the ground lies every sort of gum and discarded
pizza parlor ad as well as flyers for the Baptist barbecue

and Muslim special service. Three homeless men turn
their collars up behind the marble-columned building

that used to be a train station, blow into their hands
covered with half-gloves or none at all, walk back

and forth to keep warm and because they have
nowhere else to go but this lot I have pulled into

forty years later trying to find a place to turn
around. Forty years ago, even in summers, my father

drove me down Broad Street at 8 a.m. past the train
station, bustling back then with women and men marching

up its marble stairs, pulling hard on the heavy doors.
We rode past the graffiti-covered Jewish Theological

Seminary that always looked closed. Today
I can't find it at all. In 1968 the city knocked down

blocks and blocks of North Philly where several families
crowded into curtainless row houses with cracked

cement stoops, rusty metal railings. I remember
the morning wrecking balls and camera crews came

to Philly's poorest black ghetto where sunshine
only makes things look bleaker. My father tuned

to KYW, *all news all the time*, all local, every ten
minutes, stories breaking and repeating themselves

like soured food. Local weather and traffic followed
news of two children found tied up with duct tape

in an abandoned car while the war in Viet Nam
didn't make air time anytime on this station.

On Broad Street the lights synchronized for
or against us. At twenty five miles an hour it was

green-green-green all the way to McGonigal Hall
where my father dropped me each morning and

picked me up each afternoon barely stopping
long enough for my jacket to not get caught

in the doors' metal closing—except for
the afternoon my father got high with a hitchhiker.

Imagine a bald Jewish immigrant—who believes
he sounds like a native New Yorker, who winces if

someone calls him green-horn—driving his gold
Buick down Broad Street, sucking in the sweet

smoke, holding it in a few seconds
longer than the hitchhiker held his own.

Hear him say afterward, *How come nothing happened?*
How come I wasn't more happy or sad or hungry or

wanting to kiss anyone other than my wife?
Broad Street—with broken glass along curbs,

check-cashing stalls and bargain basements where
Slightly Damaged appeared to be a brand label—

belonged to my father and me.
My father would end up on Broad Street for months

in blue snow-flake-covered hospital gowns and
every Friday night we'd bring the blue and white box

of Sabbath candles, its lid shining with Jerusalem's
golden-domed temple, and we'd light Sabbath flames

in secret, our heads covered with kippot in all shades
of Bar Mitzvah-blue, inscribed with names of boys

my father no longer knew. In the too cold or too hot
white room we'd recite the prayer of thanks

to God for bringing us to that day, whatever day
it was, for all hours after the Holocaust were

a steal, my father used to say. We were family he
wasn't supposed to have. Every day he looked

at us with pride and dismay at what he had been
given. On Broad Street we never spoke of that.

But I knew. I knew from the way he laughed
about how the hitchhiker never suspected

he was a greenhorn who got to live
in America and drive

his daughter up and down Broad Street,
littered with hope and luck and brokenness.

Doris Ferleger

DRESS MADE IN HAIFA, 1968

My father and I trudged up three flights of cement stairs that swung around to a small shop in the back where a stout Israeli woman who spoke only to my father in Polish, Yiddish and Hebrew, all his native tongues, and hers, showed us the white linen embroidered fabric as if it were contraband. *Zeyer special,* she nodded. We nodded, she measured with string that she placed against the yard stick, she cut with no pattern, she pinned even faster than my father did in his shop, Dacron to damask, she lifted my arms sharply, but not unkindly, she fitted, and finally she looked well pleased. My father loved to buy me dresses. My father and fabric, my father and bargains, my garment-district immigrant father and his pinned-up American daughter who resembled more and more daily each of his murdered sisters. I was eighteen when I stood before the long mirror in the short white Israeli dress, where vines, made of gold shimmering beads with tiny holes bored straight through them, hung on by threads as they made a daring crossing over breasts and belly.

RHINOPLASTY AND A MIZVAH

Such a good Hebrew, he speaks.
He asks we should follow to his Arab village.
I should be chaperone, interpreter. We go. Is a mitzvah.
My father is all mischief, not dark at the moment.

The tiny house in the Druze village
of Daliyat is dark, but not a sad dark, a cool dark,
a curtain of relief from the sunburnt sky slung over
stalls and the Wailing Wall we had wept over like widows
this morning in Jerusalem. My father says the house
reminds him of the Old Country. He must mean
its smallness since every time he speaks of Poland
                    it is unbearably cold.

We drink from thimble-sized
cups, coffee thicker than cups, poured by the sister
from a samovar of bronze painted brilliant red, cobalt
blue, gemstone green with mosaic sequins. The sister's eyes,
polished chestnuts, drop their gaze toward the hand-
twined carpet, but not before you can see God
placed those eyes very close together, while her nose
God fashioned into a long hilly journey and her lips
narrow rivers parting like a shy kiss, and brow
one uninterrupted dark stream. Her hair is
covered with the white gauzy scarf
                    of tradition.

The brother stands alongside, slight,
animated, vigorously offering almonds, figs,
a walk, just the two of us, maybe to the 3rd century
synagogue in the center of his peaceful Arab village.
I like the way his hands look soft, how they shine
like unripe olives, like my father's, *Avram the schvartze,*

Doris Ferleger

Abraham the dark one, as he was known
      in the Old Country.

        The young Arab proffers dates
and proposes: *Druze and Jews we are like brothers, yes?*
Love same country, same mountains. We walk, yes?
He has been so kind. But I turn my eyes
into a thick curtain. Drawn to the sister's face,
I cannot leave her as she stands, a mirror stripped
      of all the strides I have made to hide

        our likenesses, hundreds of them—
hairs I have plucked to make my own black river
divide. Nose broken by the hit-man who saw himself
a sculptor—his hammer, file, scalpel, chiseled away
my nation's mountains, making them into valleys—
      low and profane.

        I have un-Jewed myself,
my olive-skinned beauty, I want to tell my Semite sister,
muted myself with cameo creams, tried and tried
to feel the opposite of alone. The only thing still
like hers is my blue-black hair shining,
though not the same, as it remains unbound
by tradition I long for and leave—
      at the same time.

DARK HORSE

My father is twenty and strong
as a horse when the Nazis come
to his tiny ghetto town where
he has returned to die with family,
but it turns out he's one
of the lucky ones, chosen
to heap the dead ones
into wagons so Chmielnik
could be *Judenfrei.*
The Nazis give out
numbers to the lucky ones,
numbers to count
their blessings on.
My father's number is thirteen.
After loading the last, he sees
unlucky numbers shot
up against a wall—
one-two-three—he flees—
carrying his luck in his feet.
Every March thirteenth,
my birthday, he tells me
this story. I am his lucky child,
born on his lucky number.

Before the crematoria, my father sleeps
on a straw bed next to his father and
mother. Sometimes he hears them
lovemaking. After the crematoria
they all sleep together, bound
in one swaddling, in my father's
dreams. His nightmares haunt
my dark woods and I dream a dark horse
is pulling a wooden cart up a steep

Doris Ferleger

rubble road. The cart is filled with
flattened dead foxes, all neatly arranged
like crimson sardines. I am very small,
following behind the dark
horse, the dead foxes.
Rolled in dirty rags, I carry scrolls
only a man can decipher.
A laughing woman in a flame-red-dress
is dancing on a table on the side in the road.
Bring me the scrolls, she calls.

In my childhood my father sometimes finds
himself happy. He takes me to waltz on the
yellow kitchen linoleum. One-two-three—
one-two-three, the lucky one, he carries me—
lifts me like sacred scrolls into his arms.

HIS BREATH IN MY HANDS

Today I get up real close
to my father to tell him he has to decide
to have a hole in his throat
so he can breathe,
so he can survive. He points
around the room—
wife, son, daughter—his life
by family vote—how we used to decide
what TV show to watch.
His breath in my hands.

What will you say about me
when I die? he wants to know.
We take turns. *You were funny,*
smart, good, hard-working. You never
complained about your life.
He smiles at that last one.
I didn't want to burden my family,
his eulogy in my mouth.

Doris Ferleger

CLOSE TO FATHER'S DAY

The night you lay in the metal bed
momma rented so you could die
in your own room, I whispered
into your left ear, your son
into your right,
neither of us asking after
what the other had said.
Momma had left the room
letting us believe you were still dying,
though anyone could see
your face was already grey, though
the breathing machine, still
attached to you,
kept clanking, colluding, clanking.

THE WAY DREAMS JUMP

My father's head is a lopsided black
and white blob, out of focus, the face
wiggly like chilling Jell-o when you check on it
too soon. Hitchcock shadows streak
across his once fleshy cheeks, his still
globular nose, his shiny head, then slow down
as if looking for a place to land, but they don't.

When his face finally sets, it doesn't
have eyes like giant winter-green
gum-balls, that dumfounded look,
the classic Shy-Drager Syndrome stare
only one female intern recognized, just like that,
her first night on call. Now they're
basset hound eyes. For months he lay
on that crunchy plastic-covered mattress,
stiff as the unnerving white sheets, or else
he sat raggedy, floppy like a doll that's lost
its stuffing, his head and torso hanging
sideways over the arm of a stupid
green chair, its legs cold metal,
always shiny. The nurses minded
their own business.

Wheeling himself into my dream-
garden of bonsai, my father doesn't seem
to notice the unlikeliness of his presence
here where everything continues
to be small, controlled, cut just so,
where trunks and limbs of raft-style bonsai
mimic giant trees felled by erosion,
beating winds, other natural disasters.

Doris Ferleger

Each fallen tree in my dream-garden
re-plants itself just by lying there,
three or more new trunks growing straight
from the side of the felled trunk that faces
upward, while the side kissing the dirt
sends down new roots.
Imagine being the only one left
growing roots that turn
into family you get to feed
and love.

PRAYING TO A STONE

Talking to God is like talking to a stone,
Momma muses while you doze.
Prayer helps like leeches
on a dead person, Aunt Nadia adds.

Cousin Frieda admits she still prays,
though not to God, but to her mother,
because her mother promised
she'd answer: *Listen for me, Friedele.*

Momma says: *I was the youngest of ten*
and prayed to no one, even before the war.
All I wanted back then were warm boots,
pretty plucked eyebrows, a piece of chicken.
In ghetto we had plenty loose bricks
but nothing to hide behind them.
Not one zloty to put under a walnut shell.
Now so many zlotys. Helps like wet rags.

While you lay in your hospital bed,
did you hear us? Or were you remembering
your living grave, fifty years before,
where you hid under hay and dirt, rough plank,
clicks of Nazi boots? Seeing you
in that hospital bed, imprisoned
in your own body, in your own thoughts,
permanently attached to tubes
you couldn't rip out, able to see our hands
but not reach for them, I admit to times
I prayed for your death. Momma, god of iron,
pressed her comb through your random hairs,

Doris Ferleger

her kisses onto your eyes and each
of your unmoving fingers. God,
wet in Momma's kisses and combing,
did it feel like swallowing a stone?

PART 2: CONFISCATIONS

CONFISCATIONS

I can't really wait to finish
all the sad poems in paradise
before I write to you, dear thief,
who assigned this slow-reading
heart to write freely, or did you say free,
of my simple shtetl, my surviving mother
whose still buttery skin and flagging eyes
grow wider with each new body part aching
to fail. You would think she'd be accustomed
by now, to illness's overtures to dying,
having seen one sister forgetting for years
the English word for sister, the other sister
turning her own grief into disbelief, disgust;
it was easier that way. *Whatcha talking?*
You can't walk like a mensch with normal steps?
Chimyshe! Hold yourself up!

Momma was changing
Aunt Alice's sheets in the hospital the day
I came to sing death songs to her
watery yellow sclera of eyes.
Momma had taken up a sort of low-
residency in that hospital until the day
Alice's eyes popped open and froze
like that forever, her mouth also locked open
like the terror of the moon, the jaw stuck
like that, in my eyes, for years, until
a healer told me to see her holding
an egg, mist, a tower.

As if that were not enough,
father's illness came next, mute years of

his wanting to die before every organ
shorted out the way bladder and lungs
had already. And there were
of course momma's memories of cities
and bodies burning sixty years before.
After the war momma felt safe
from death and there were just
too many to mourn. Now she barely
sleeps so she won't close her eyes for good.

I have spent lots of money on therapy
so as not to sit inside her skin, not to
scratch at the sight of her psoriasis or
search for the perfect salve to smear
on my head, I mean her head,
not to be eating mashed peas from jars
and applesauce to make the pain
pills slide down easy in her throat.
Last night in the ER I had to look away
each time she tried to take a deep breath,
assuring her short ones were just fine,
my own breath spastic, jumpy.

I used to seek solace from my mother,
though maybe it was more a kind of
worry by proxy I sought and found.
When Max's mother died he said
now there was no one surviving
who would care if he ever
brushed his teeth again.
In a fat book called *The Corrections*,
the line that stays with me is when
the mother gets told by her doctor

Doris Ferleger

she looks *youthful* and she thinks
he is saying she looks *useful*
so she lights up.

These days my mother is seduced
hourly by each of her body's
throbbings and tendernesses
that make her forgo the past, though
just yesterday she told my husband,
Still every time I take a shower
my breath gets chopped off, like
from the inside. Why?
What a question. Showers in the camps
were not so good, you know, meaning
her nakedness was always a sign
of waiting for the gas.

DEAR BILL

You tell me to cross out
all the vampire imagery I keep
holding up to depict the sucking
out of life force but I keep feeling
water-clear blood being pumped
out through a long slow plastic tube
from the most apparent vein
in my inner elbow crease,
the daughter's life force shifting
into the mother's feeding tube
while the daughter hungers for
something thicker than the super-
alimentation entering the mother's body.

So I do away with all that blood
imagery and go off
to my Chinese medicine doctor
to treat my depleted state—my yin-
deficient kidney point—
did I say my mother has a tumor
growing on her kidney and one
on her lung? She says she knows
a man who lived for fifteen years
with one lung, another who got even
more years out of one kidney.

Every body is constituted
of ineffable chemical bonds,
my doctor argues; there is no metaphor
other than the vampire here in the West
for the age old mother-
daughter bond gone

Doris Ferleger

haywire when the mother is close
to dying and starts like a newborn
to suck. The daughter feels empty,
not drained but unusually free
of guilt. Even shame—when everything
inside feels like bones
too broken to be made whole—
is missing. A steady trickle of
some unfamiliar substance, she blots
with plush resentments and the Zen paradox:
Live as if you were already
dead—so there will be no separation
anxiety.

Stretching out
her white arm, my doctor
milks an imaginary
plastic tube. It isn't just
a metaphor, it's an understatement
for small-scale annihilations
caused by too much
wind or not enough
metal.

NEED

In *non-violent communication*
you state your observation, make
a feeling statement about that observation,
then you say, *This is what I need
from you.* It must be a need
that the other person can fulfill
now or in the future, but he or she has
a choice about fulfilling it at all.
Like, *I need to feel appreciated.
Would you be willing to make a few,
that is, three or four,
appreciative comments some time
this week?* I'm not sure
if I have this right,
as I am still unable to swallow
this notion of need.

Need—a grotesque protrusion of an aberrant nature,
puce-colored with odd, almost wart-like nubs growing
in profusion over the protrusion—highly aggressive
with monstrous possibilities
of taking over, of giving pleasure,
as in ahh, a need fulfilled.

Need—a shaming experience, known to occur
most commonly among humans, especially in regard to:
the need to exist, the need to breathe
through the bottom of the throat,
through the esophagus,
through the whole circle of rib cage,
to whisper; the need to be alone,
to love without disappearing; the need to be

Doris Ferleger

seen, to be known, to be limited,
aka human; the need to know
one's limitations,
the need to speak them.

*

Spit me out, spit me out!
My Hebrew teacher used to hold out
his hand in front of our mouths and wait
for the gum we were chewing
and mean it, his face showing
not even a hint of disgust.

*

My spiritual teacher gave a new meditation
this week on need, any need
I can't chew, can't spit out, find
disgusting, I say, *This*
too, this too I swallow.

*

How do I say,
I observe, I feel, I need—
without needing
to be dying
to say it?

LEAVING UNTOUCHED

I admit I want to be left
alone with my sore
throat and urgent
bladder, to read
great poems about God
and death, not to be
called to discuss
strategies for what
to do if the needle
aimed and guided
into our mother's lung
tumor the size of a
pinkie fingernail ends
up killing her. I am
sorry to have left you
alone with that needle
and our mother
bleeding as she was
inside yet strangely
calm outside. So unlike her
to be unvigilant.
Perhaps your vigilance
felt enough
like her own. I admit I
want to be left
writing on the strangeness
of this time, neither sad
nor scared nor, at the moment,
angry. I finish my plate
of strawberries, leaving
untouched only their green
crowns and stiff stems
that point at me

Doris Ferleger

accusingly. You call to say,
Doris, sixty percent of people
with lung cancer die
within a year, Doris,
it's eighty percent for eighty-
something-year-olds like
our mother. A few red
tear-shaped berries
are left in the blue bowl
in the fridge, but my taste
for them is gone as you
repeat my name before
each new statistic, as if
you're taking my face
in your hands through
the phone wires and turning
it toward you
without touching. My heart
turns wild in my chest
despite my desire to be done
with this way of sparring
when all I want is something
we never had. I ask if you know
the numbers of
survivors of Auschwitz,
of Chmielnik's genocide,
what percent is 10,000
one day, turned to
150 the next? I hate how
you use the numbers
to set off familiar
familial alarms. I don't remember

you doing that before. It was
our mother's job to
warn us with worse
case scenarios. It took me
years to stop
believing I was just
about to fall.
I am sorry to leave you
alone. Our parents,
if they had counted
themselves among the
eighty percent, would
have lain down at the side
of the road, lifted each
other's faces for a last
kiss, and let all the best
stolen potatoes roll away.

Doris Ferleger

PART 3: FIT-FOR-LIFE

FIT-FOR-LIFE

I used to think I could live
on air and certain plants and fruits if I had lived
in the time of the Holocaust for which
I now understand I was unwittingly practicing.

Medical science says starving strips
a person of her wits quicker than hard drugs;
the brain becomes unable to receive
love or essential information. Momma says
I would have keeled over in a week
of the death marches; that's how it was,
comparing myself always to the impossible
tasks in the brown shadows on the roads
of war constructed from dirt since childhood.

New studies show rats live longer
on starvation diets, and men and women in their sixties
are taking this hypothesis and running
like rats on wheels in cages that smack of metal-
bladed experiments once conducted on my kind.
And the necks of the fit-for-life, tucked-in
or saggy-skinned, are white as rats since
survival of the fittest also involves
avoidance of sun, and *death*
shall have no dominion.

My brother, who first played me Dylan
Thomas' Hades-haunting voice, says the reason
he doesn't exercise is that it's too hard
to hike with the weight of all those oranges and
I laugh knowing exactly what the heaviness
of oranges has to do with our common childhoods,
starvations we never suffered but did,

in-case-of-war food we didn't need to carry
but did, and I reveal to him the weight
of my suitcase filled with yeast-free bread
exceeding the limits when I flew to Poland
to visit Auschwitz, our mother's alma mater.

Once it was nuns who conducted fasts
for *enlightenment*; no pun is ever intended.
I too was looking for God
but didn't expect to find Him
between two slices of whole wheat bread.
For years I lived on rice cakes, choosing
the ones with the highest air content.
My brother is too fat and I, too lean
and our mother still complains about
our bodies not being just right to live
through the war successfully.

Doris Ferleger

TANTA HOYNA

For Sarah Paul, of blessed memory

In mine Hungary, daarrlink,
was like dis:
I watched mine best friend
running into mine house,
I thought to say goodbye to me.

I was sure she didn't see
I was on the truck already
and if I called to her
they would kill me.
This I knew.

Then I saw her running
with mine best dress, a red velvet
with a black satin collar
she always liked to try on
and I was thinking,

oh, she did see me
and she is risking her life
to give me mine dress
my mother made for me.
But I see she is laughing
and she is looking
at me in the truck
and she is calling me,
you know, haunney,
what she called me?
Dirty, you know, *Jew*.

You see mine daughter
over there, daarrlink?
A beautiful girl, no?
When we come from Israel
inside Philadelphia, America,

I make her such a dress,
she wears to school first day,
but mine daughter comes home
crying, the teacher put her on
such a ugly yellow hat made from

destruction paper, looked
like ice cream cone turned over
on her head, made her sit in a corner,
told the other kids to call her
stupid, since she couldn't speak
English. You know me, haunney.
I *shlepped* mine daughter back
to that *fashtunkina* school,
walked up to Mrs. Smarty-pants

and started in Hebrew, then Hungarian,
last in English. In Amerrica, I said,
we have refrigerator, washing machine,
doctor. Now we have teacher.
So we sit with you
and you teach us de English
so we don't be called stupid anymore.

Doris Ferleger

Haunney, I tell you something,
even after such things like this
I never want to live anywhere
but Amerrica. Yesterday I turned
fifty and you know what I did?

I put on mine shortest dress,
mine highest heels, mine sunglasses,
and walked down Booselton Avenue until
I counted up a few good whistles.
Then, I went home and baked
mine special mun cookies.

You know *mun*, poppy seeds,
live even when you don't think
is possible. Underground for years,
then, hup, they pop up! Who would believe?
Mine Jewish *mun* in America!

A GOD'S EYE

Neti! neti! Not this! Not that!
Nothing is God. We can't have
a God's eye view, no matter where
we stand. We're like the five
blind brothers
trying to describe the elephant
to their blind father,
one standing at the pink underbelly
of the ear saying, *the elephant is*
flat and soft as mashed banana.
We can't see why some get to live
through random bullets, freak
accidents, genocides, while still
others get to see the crimson
cardinal landing right
in front of their eyes, while
four million slaves in India
owe money to the man
and their children will also
owe, be slaves,
go hungry and so on. I eat
more pineapples than anyone
I know. Pineapples grow where
crops are for export only
so I guess I've been stealing
unwittingly from slaves.
I am frankly bored with my
guilt, and clichés about karma
don't help either. *Neti! Neti*!
Not this! Not that! Guilt
has nothing to do with
the bobolink, the whippoorwill,
the snow-cricket, the beetle, or grief
stalking the beetle.

Doris Ferleger

DOORS AND WINDOWS

This is my modest gift to the Jewish people who have always dreamt of biblical love, friendship and of peace among all peoples...to that people which lived here thousands of years ago among the other Semitic people... All the time I was working, I felt my mother and father looking over my shoulder; and behind them were Jews, millions of other vanished Jews of yesterday and a thousand years ago. —Marc Chagall, 1962

No matter how hard I
close the doors
there are always people
leaving. No one can get out of
the airport but they don't
know it yet, so they're not frantic,
only I am. Somehow
the glass doors
finally open, something
I've done, maybe
I've stepped out
of bounds or into the eye
of the camera that's connected
to something that is moved
by the sight of
human beings. Running
electricity makes us believe
we are running things.
A dog, small and jaunty,
miniature boxer, trots right
through the doors, leaving
the airport without a hitch,
he's on his own
in his sleek brown coat, fancy
silver collar, not belonging
to the elderly man
who follows close behind,

who thanks me for
letting him through. I don't
know what I've done
to deserve his thanks.

*

This window I have drawn
on the blackboard called
the Johari Window is divided,
as you can see, into four panes
that are not really equal.
Pane four holds all things
others don't know
about you and you don't
even know about yourself.
Pane number three encloses
all the things others see
about you that you don't see
about yourself, like the True Mirror
that lets you see yourself
the way others see you. I see myself
the wrong way every day.
No matter what I cover
the windows with, people
are always seeing
through me.

*

At the bottom of my dream
I discover a device that
measures what each person needs
to feel close to another. Alive again
my father is sitting happily

Doris Ferleger

on the right side
of the synagogue. He never sat
on the right side, always the left,
near the twelve Chagall Windows,
twelve sons blessed by Joseph in Genesis,
twelve tribes blessed by Moses in times
when a father's blessing was
already causing trouble
and forefathers should have known
better than to call us
chosen. In the twelve windows
you can see everything
each person needs
to feel close to her true nature:
doves and eagles soar and swoop
under stars and seasons; stag and lion
leap over Sabbath flames; figs and flowers
flourish, and open
human hands reach out in brilliant
pigments veneered together
for the first time in history,
many different colors on one
uninterrupted pane of glass,
no longer needing to be separated
by cold strips of metal.
Emerald, sapphire, beryl, lapis lazuli,
jasper swirl like the sea on the twelve
windows, twelve colors
to remind us of the twelve gemstones
gleaming on the High Priest's
breast-plate that covers the heart,
yet still lets through its light,
its invisible electricity.

FACING

Six days
after her big surgery,
I visit Sophie
at Presby.
Her lips turn up
at the corners
permanently now
and the doctor worked
in the trenches
in her cheeks, filling them up
real puffy, like two
flawless sponge cakes.
Sophie said she had longed
to look the way she did
before going through
the year watching
her husband whittle
away, the cancer carving
too slowly. She said,
The year has felt like trees
falling on my face.
She said, I don't really like
this new face either. She said,
It doesn't match
how I mourn.

Doris Ferleger

OH SAGE

1.

Luna, your two sets of eyes—
I will fail you
when I speak of you—
how you let me watch these
death throes beating
your green wings
that contain all
your eyes open
on your back—watch
how you flip over into surrender,
show the white-white of your belly
that appears to made of sweet
crystal clumping or spongy naphtha
that kills you. A dark crust
like a thumbnail of baked phyllo
pops off your crystalline belly.
When I tell this in the only
failed way I can, Yvette says
this may have been your cache of eggs
left at the end, at the side of the road—
and your wings I watched gasping
last breath after last breath until
I thought I couldn't bear
any more beauty alone.

2.

Oh sage of all sages, were you
watching the impossible
day our neighbor Barbara
walked up the three flights

of stairs from her apartment
to ours, stood in a choking
shade of blue, arms raised
high over her head
as she fell into my arms,
as she let go the last
particles of her supper,
leaving me there
to hold her bones, fat, flesh
the soul always leaves
to the care of failures?
Some say I was chosen
to watch so she would not be
alone in her dying
as she had been in her living,
surrendered as she was to that
singular tray table, that one pale leg
of chicken, oily and tepid.

3.

An animal is ready to die
only after looking
into it's predator's eyes until
they both see themselves
as one weeping.

Doris Ferleger

SPELL TO BE SAID UPON HEARING THE PAIN OF A LOVED ONE

Owl eyes, steady on the tree line,
sheen of winter in the valley.
Who will sing to you a lullaby of
living and dying into this river,
of suffering into this pale blue day?
Who will carry meat to your cave?

Who will carry meat to your cave,
meat for singing,
cusp of hollow light?
No need. Small risk,
this speaking wind.
Scarlet, this emptying stream.

Doors turning into stairways.
Continue forward, lying here,
in this final straw bed, holding
only magnolia petals, dropping
only magnolia petals as you leave.

No one will. All will. Mourn,
old owl eye, my heart.
Sing from where you fly, dropping
petals into rivers.

NOT GIVING

In Chinese medicine the bladder is all
about cleverness—not giving, not kindness.
My Chinese doctor says I am very resourceful
at giving, but I must start holding onto,
with all my might, like the basketball
my son steals and hugs raw, grunts and pivots,
his face red and sweaty. I am also good

at gratitude, but it's not enough to be grateful
for tiny brown seeds that form
flowers when you cut
slice after slice of the kiwi,
green wafers on the tongue;
for fresh basil's satisfying bitterness;
for raspberry, shaped like a cup
for the tip of the tongue
to enter, tiny globes popping with juices;

for a woman I had known for decades, knew her
dreams and the shape of her feet, yet
when she asked what I would write of her life,
all I could remember was the raspberry, its dark
red seeds catching in her teeth and the wind
against the window of the train, her breath
making a small circle of fog
as she pronounced the name
of her city *Varshava*.

She wanted me to remember
more than I did, to love
more than I did.
But that one raspberry
is all I can remember, the way she held it
like something stolen
or saved.

Doris Ferleger

FLOODING AND FLOATING

As human suffering floods New Orleans
one face speaks on the evening news.
Elderly, black, no family, she lay
for eight days on her mattress

floating in fetid brown water,
scanning her drifting possessions,
guessing at what would endure,
what would not.

Painted bureau, pink floral dishes,
red satin-lined jewel box that made her
think of Linda Sue from the shopper's
channel, and led her to imagine calling:

This is Melba from Looziana. Yes, I survived
just fine. The Diamoniques—all those sparkles—
washed away. Won't it be a lucky day
for the gal who finds them?

Melba thought of her favorite TV lovers,
cheaters, heiresses, victims, villains,
her only daily companions—
missing.

When asked what saved her life, she says,
There must have been a lot of wood
in that mattress: it floated just like Noah's ark.
Melba said she wasn't afraid even once.

Picture cattle and chickens floating
down the streets and wonder, of what fabric
did God fashion Melba? What diamond
glisten kept her alive and believing?

Envision the oil lamp in the ancient temple
burning for eight days with only enough oil
for one, and suddenly know—
Melba lit that lamp with the glint of her eye

See Noah cramped inside the ark with the zebras,
hippos, skunks, floating forty days and forty nights.
Spot the dove returning, announcing dry land,
holding Melba's faith fresh in its mouth.

Doris Ferleger

RUNNING FREE

For Lilly and Samara

Now the crashing
into the first tower.
Crashing into the second
yet to come. Time between
crashes is everlasting time
as my Mara rides the subway
from Bed Sty to the Village
for class, as the subway halts
between stops and white tile walls
shine close on either side,
as passengers are told:
Go above ground, now!
As my Mara doesn't yet
know from what she's escaping,
as she climbs the piss-ripe
cement stairs seeking safety
in the smutty island air,
as she arrives street level, as her eyes
shoot up just in time
to see the second tower
smote down, *the demolition
of her youth.* She calls it that.

Mara eats no meat, no
chicken, nothing that needs
to be killed in order
for her to live.
It started when
she was three and lisped,
*Mommy, tsicken
is tsicken!* Meaning what
was on her plate was

just yesterday
running free
in our neighbors' yards.

Doris Ferleger

TO TRY AGAIN

For R.

Almost bearable, this body,
unbearable the weight of this
snow cover
thick as love's absence
on a spring day
when you have lost
the one you have slept
and eaten with longer than
three childhoods,
too bearable, this hair-shirt
you're told to wear to show
you're mourning though
you know the sun will scorch
your skin like the burnt offering, the field
you will be, the field that will remember
nothing, lay fallow for a year,
remember how the corn roots feel
in the soil, some human hand
must do the planting—
to try again.

AFTER I UNDERSTOOD THE SEA

I am the sane sister
who writes poems in Aramaic,
eats mangoes and pomegranate seeds, sings
to the earnest ocean that sings back—
I am God's daughter, God's blueness
born in me, God's teal, God's aqua,
yellow and cerulean fish, God's eel and barracuda,
God's pelicans standing like sentries—

there is nothing like them, blending into brown
sand cliff faces where red-headed cacti grow
quilled and puckered, cherubic and juicy
inside crevasses, and when the moment is right—
wham! They come swooping down—
three or four at a time—nosedive—
cracking blue water
like freedom bells.

Some would have you believe
I am the insane sister
because of my fishy eyes,
wide and lidless, because I left him
under the sweet fig tree, traveled to the sea
cliffs and scrub—became fisher and weaver,
crossing threads, warp and weft.

At every cross-hatch an ache of wanting—
where ribs meet—this is the warp
from which Adam was taken
from my breast
bone. Yes, Adam
was taken from here, and for so long
I grieved his going, though he would say

Doris Ferleger

I am the one who left,
and I did, but only later, after
I understood the sea
would be forbidden
as well as the fruit.

WITHOUT REMEMBERING

Twelve geese fly over the river in oscillating
V formation, both geese and sky reaching
a different kind of victory. The sun gives
herself freely and takes half back. The river I want you
to see and feel and hear and smell runs with neither
ache nor joy. On still days it turns from
brown to olive green, though you will not
see it turning. It looks all surface
until you see the fishermen standing
in grey-green rubber boots
up to their hips, no words, only the arcs
of their lines being tossed
and the denseness of water
around their legs. You don't see
the breathing fish. If you're lucky, you'll see
the wood ducks that look painted and one-
dimensional and have a red streak and unblinking eyes.

 To tell you of the river without remembering, I bend
my knees before you, open my hands
full of desire and feel a shimmering
that is neither joy nor ache nor fear
nor knowledge. Nothing
I remember has prepared me for this.
I do not remember ever trusting this much.

Doris Ferleger

IF ALL IS GOD

If all is God—why opposites—
why sun blinding still air—
why *tsimsum*—complete
withdrawal
of light?
If all is one
light poured into a thousand
vessels each the color of cobalt
and the Dead Sea—
if we are all one
light scattered into the void
when our vessels are shattered—
who shattered us?
(If you loved me you wouldn't.)
If we are shattered
how are we already
whole? Is our longing
for wholeness
wholeness itself?
If we are made
of one light,
why do we appear
only a fragment
of light? If each is a bead
on a long God-necklace—
pearl, Conus shell, bone,
sea glass—tossed at the whim
or discernment of waves
turning over each piece
like obsessive thought —
how each of us suffers
though we are already whole—

then why do I seek
to shame you
(if I loved you I wouldn't),
to blame you—
love of my life
who makes me whole?
If we are made of God—
of what is God
ashamed?
Why do we not
both cry out
as one—who can say
to another
love of my life
who shatters me—
who makes me whole—

Doris Ferleger

PART 4: TOUCH FALLING

SCARED

None of us ever asked my father
if he was scared all those months
he lay dying. Max, who writes
self-help books for men says
men are scared most of the time
even when not dying.

Last night our son spoke to me
in a bristly tone but it didn't
scrape me down this time. I just
said *whoa*, like that, a big *whoa*
came out of me in one short punching
breath. He stopped, even nodded.
My mouth felt like it could
blow away rock-coral.
A mad wind died down
to rest on the trees
outside our kitchen window.

My husband says
nothing at times like that which
still makes me mad. He tells me
he's silent because I'm
strong and smart and can speak for
myself just fine. Besides,
he loves us both and sees
both sides. But I long for him
to throw the pointed
look my father gave
for the slightest scent of
surliness toward momma.

My husband says
men are scared of women swallowing
them up which is why he's afraid to call me
his bear the way our spiritual teacher
told him to. Imagine how easily
the honey goes down. *Seriously,*
my husband says, *women can eat
us up*, which means if he announced
at the dinner table
how he adores me he might feel
like an animal
surrendering all.
Even after all these years
of loving each other so hard
the winds have blown in every direction
through us, even after
all the years of repairing
what the winds in us destroyed.

Doris Ferleger

WEIGHTED

I feels his absence
at the dinner table tonight
though he is sitting right beside me
speaking of his childhood, his mother
and father each holding
their own, only barely, while he
shaved down pennies into dimes
for vending machines, especially
for the Mars Bars,
and the neighbor lady fed him
Chiclets as if he were
a baby bird. Weighted
with the kind of silence that feeds
no one, that leaves
no room for me to enter,
I make puns. I hate
puns. I am bad at puns. *Honey*
bear forbearers with forbearance.
If he ever called me his honey-
bear maybe I would be scared
of knowing how big I am,
how we each need
the other as much as sky,
or maybe I would
be more kind.

CROCUS

Fortunate, you are,
white as baby's new tooth
opening.

And what about the man who thumbs seedlings
into earth, who coaches emerald shoots pouring up
around the slow-creeping clematis,
deep purple suns,

the man who loves his garden,
who lies down with me in the folding night air
when cicada love calls
crescendo and cool?

If we are fortunate, he will be planting beside me
when you appear again as if
out of a child's mouth.

Doris Ferleger

WHOOSH

It's night and he becomes
afraid of sleep as well
as sleeplessness. He wants
to feel only a steady
softness in his chest instead of
these flagrant beats, instead of this
vulnerable. At the slightest
pull, he thinks of his father, healthy
as a horse until he stopped
breathing, suddenly
keeled over and whoosh—
was gone at the exact
age this man is today,
his fifty seventh year
beginning. This morning
he hears a turtle dove and dreams
of saving his wife
from the apocalypse as she sleeps,
both of them so light
in sleep that it doesn't feel
anything like death,
except sometimes.

TOUCH FALLING

For God, I searched among the high reeds and found Moses' missing brothers weeping in the Nile's tributaries. Wading in marshes up to my knees, I found women flailing husks against wood, winnowing the paddy rice against Cambodia's displaced wind. Fallen rivers and old close trees I found everywhere and human hands and goodness, and baskets and more baskets, floating with flaws of men and God—and women still looking to men to be God's completeness—and women looking up from their disappointment, seeing only the last disappearing sparks of what had fallen, sparks that looked like stars and excruciating kisses, excruciating because they could only hint at what had been missed, excruciating because if they had been felt, they would have burned like Vermont lake water, a coldness that sears though the body is blue and shivering. I admit, along the lake, the luna moth died without my touch, that I touched its sage green wing only after it turned to excruciating spark and kiss. I admit that I failed to touch it while it was still alive because I am afraid of God's fragility. Because in the touch, all expectation ends. One must feel only what is ablaze in that moment. Your touch, my darling, falling in red and blue arches onto my whole ready skin, makes me unready for death, no matter how I try to prepare, polishing myself against you.

Doris Ferleger

BIG SILENCES IN A YEAR OF RAIN

1.

                In Belgium I lived with big silences
a year of rain couldn't drown out and a desk my groom built of six-
by-six particle board, the only piece of furniture in the whole
living room, he painted white—the desk on which he drew lungs,
liver, femur, large and small muscle groups, intestines, spleen
in three dimensions, deeper, larger than our lives together,
a cardboard box full of colored pencils sharpened into
meticulous points when otherwise we were both unable
to make ourselves cheerful or understood.

Truth be told, I'm jealous of your husband, said my G-Y-N,
seventy, shaky, forgetful, giving me the wrong sized dome
of protection right before I left. *Studying anatomy in Europe
means your husband will know by heart even the location
of body parts that have become extinct! How romantic,
your first year of marriage in Europe!*

People to this day, thirty years later, say that. I tell them
it wasn't, never failing to mention the ninety days
straight of rain and the surprise party my husband
threw for me at Bert's place with real live American
deli food and sesame bagels which sounds great, right,
until I sigh and say all I had wanted, all I had been
planning for, all year was to go out for our first
romantic dinner together on my birthday. I had even
decided months before on the chocolate
suede skirt despite its too tight, too heavy fabric, more
cumbersome than sexy. My husband, trying so hard
to please, even lied with stories like *I gotta go help Bert move
his bed* when he was really working out paper plates
and Motown for me, Clapton for him and Stella Artois

for everyone, leaving me feeling rather troubled when
he said I didn't have to dress up so much or at all really.

Don't get me wrong, I am sure my husband loved me
in the way a twenty-four-year old— driven by ambition,
by those who told him he could do whatever he set
his mind to, and by the ones who warned he'd end up
dead at twenty-six or at least a delinquent—
could love, though I didn't know him in these ways.
I just knew he ran like a cheetah, did triple flips off
the high dive, studied dictionaries for the MCATS,
ate lots of vegetables and spoke so softly
and *highfalutinly* that my mother said,
He's nice but I don't understand a word he says.

I omit the night—that uniquely-breezy-perfect-weather
night in Belgium when my groom would have only needed
his one sports jacket with the suede elbow patches, but
instead sent me to the school play with a too tall,
too handsome fellow teacher, his thick brown hair
bunched in trenches of curls. It was Viet Nam years
and death was never far away, even with no TV or radio,
and somehow any place not Viet Nam seemed safe
and innocent and disarming. And my husband even
brought out my blue lace wrap from the falling-apart
armoire, its hinges always coming loose, not the beautiful
heavy European kind of armoire I would have loved,
the kind with sturdy fat claws for feet, but one made
like the desk, from particle board, which is really smashed-
to-pieces-waste-wood and shavings glued together,
disguised with a thin veneer of sleek teak, his mother's
favorite kind of wood. My husband even told us
to have a good time and I was certain that when I returned

Doris Ferleger

I'd find my groom poring over body parts and his French and
English dictionaries, still seated at his six-by-six desk
that was, to my eyes, a grave looking thing,

though for him that desk was a beautiful, beating body
of knowledge, a lush landscape alive with possibility.
And though nothing happened with the too tall teacher
and my husband was, in fact, drawing a femur while finishing off
the last of the Fig Newtons, there was a shift
in the tectonic plates under the country in which
I found myself. Tectonic plates move horizontally
only inches per year, yet transform boundaries of countries,
and cause continents to drift undetectably away
from each other. I didn't understand, nor did my groom, that
what we longed for were larger faults, *fracture zones* that
relieve seismic tension, connect trenches together,
even though the connections may cause massive collisions.

On that drifting continent, loneliness was nothing
to speak of between newlyweds; I couldn't imagine
saying I missed my mother or anyone—
the myths of marriage, its happily ever, its *Father-
Knows-Best*, dug deep inside my unquiet country,
and no matter how much I hated the war
we went for, I couldn't say I missed my old life
in America with young men dying daily while
war brides took up knitting or surviving back home.

The weekend a snake hissed its tongue between my legs
in World's End, was my first camping trip, my first
bacon, my first time waiting for God to strike me down
for the bacon and the first time my future husband told me

his draft number was high but warned me not to fall
in love with him anyway because he was leaving
for Belgium where med school was free, and medicine
was his first commitment, his passion. Then he began
tracing all my body parts to memorize where his heart was
until the day he could trust it to open without breaking.

2.

My husband spoke French superbly, having spent
the year before with a humming-bird-like, green-eyed
beauty named Monique, also a med student, who sat
beside her mother for eight hours on Lufthansa
all the way to America, the summer of my marriage
to Steven to find out which way the wind blew in
the land of the free. No commitments had been made
in any direction, so none could be broken; and until
Monique's arrival, Steven and I had pretended that
yet another year apart wouldn't make or break our
uncommitted-every-summer-back-together-for-three-
years-doing-back-flips-at-the-Jersey-shore relationship.

In addition to Monique's exploratory visit,
there was the black and silver circle pin that
my not-yet-groom gave me in June that bore
no special meaning—that made my father take up
arms against the man I loved, though I hadn't yet
allowed myself to even call it love, since, who knew
what wars, what annihilations lay ahead, which is
how a child of Holocaust survivors thinks;
make no plans because God is, at heart, empty-
hearted. On the other hand my father, a benevolent
patriarch from the Old Country, was known to be

Doris Ferleger

full of heart, someone to seek out for counsel on
love and clever business moves, though you
never knew when the veil of war's lost darkness
would curtain his face. My father's inner wars,
enemies, victims, were fathomless, but his battles
with others were subtle and restrained unless
the situation at hand required him to become
as large as he was on the inside, like on the night
of the farewell dinner for Steven.

       Stevele, as my father affectionately
called him, *now is time for a good walk; I get*
my last cigarette for the night,; you get your exercise;
Stevele, you and your exercise and all those bottles
of vitamins—gonna live forever. They walked.
My father blew smoke rings. *So Stevele,*
what are your intentions with my daughter?
The out-of-the-blueness, the Old World
fatherliness of the question tossed like a casual
grenade toward Steven who, lacking experience
with this kind of war, used the only ammunition he had:
It's none of your business, to which my father replied,
Stevele, until it's your business, it's my business.

Steven reported all this to me in his perfect
French, in the back seat of my parents' car on the ride
home to my parents' house where I still slept
in my floral flannels, where my same knickknacks—
pale blue Spaniels, white porcelain cats, one blue-jay
tweeting on a fence, all appeared calm, self-possessed,
on the pristine shelves above my girl-sized white desk
that sat between the twin beds in the room that was
all mine, though my mother vacuumed it, hung up

my clothes and there was no way to lock the door
since my mother believed in eminent domain
and imminent emergencies. When did I stop

putting the knickknacks to bed? When did I
stop covering them with pastel tissues,
baby pinks, greens and blues that came in family-
sized, multi-colored boxes? I was comforted
by every color, made them into giant flowers
held together in the center by pipe-cleaners.
What I am trying to say is that Steven wasn't
ready to marry, to make a commitment to a woman
who, having no desire to lie down on that bed
of official wifeliness, refused to iron his silver
cowboy shirt with the long black fringe,
the first and last time he asked, didn't cook
except for the one curried chicken dish
his mother had taught to wow any guests
with its full cup of heavy cream, spent
her days preparing lectures on literature as it
reflects the human condition, impressed with
what she imagined she knew. A woman who didn't
find the idea of living in Belgium to be romantic
or the thought of becoming a doctor's wife to be
a fantastic fantasy seeking fulfillment.

If anything, I had pictured myself living in an
unmoving black and white photo of married life
with someone satisfied to be alone, like Rodin's
The Thinker, posing hand to chin, left elbow
to right knee, permanently crouched
yet comfortable in an inner struggle

Doris Ferleger

that would never be resolved. I didn't understand
The Thinker wasn't meant to stand, alone.

What I am trying to say is that I wasn't ready either,
that my need for being blanketed while pretending
otherwise was larger than I can admit to even now,
that Steven never did propose, nor did I, that
the back seat of my parents' car was flooded
with Monique and her mother, with the ocean
they had crossed to find their answer, the ocean that
would once again divide us, Steven and me,
for another year. Flooded, with my father's question,
Steven's answer. It felt as though a huge leaden
wave was about to come and knock down what we
had built and breathed together over three years
of tapes and letters limned with Steven's loneliness,
his learning to be alone, the largest of his new-
found-friends, the Sunday dinners with those friends
who turned out to be Monique's family
welcoming him into family—and he needed family,
especially one woven tightly, one that loosened
him up on strolls among giant trees in Bois de Cambre.

In the back seat of my parents' car, I felt dropped
into border zones that belonged to both of us
yet neither of us, like the borders of countries,
not the way they look on a map—thin black lines
that separate yet show connection, but how they feel—
like the flatness of no-man's land,
narrow as a bike path but thousands of miles long,
a place where people lose each other without meaning to.

Maybe I thought marriage would mean a sharing of
loneliness, since that's what I saw in my house, though
I didn't actually see it, only picked up the sound of it
dropping out from the bottoms of things.
Maybe Steven and I were each afraid of being family
to the other, since *family*, for me, meant body parts
falling like leaves the color of lead and gun-metal
and bombs dropping through shocked trees.

And for him, well, it meant doors locking him
out or in, either way the doors swung, *family*
meant a different set of dangers, of disillusionments,
the details of which I must omit, because they weigh
too heavily on everything that matters to him,
everything he couldn't stand to lose or find again.
And for all these reasons, we attended our wedding
on Labor Day just four weeks after my father
popped the question. Steven attended the way one
attends his own funeral, because it couldn't happen
without him. In the wedding photos Steven's father
looks like the cat who swallowed a canary, his father
having been the first to think me grand; my father
looks like the man inhaling his last cigarette
before the firing squad; Steven looks straight into
the eye of the camera through his smoked
glasses under his furrowed brow, while I am looking
up at him adoringly, or so it appears. I am not saying
I was any more in love, but that my fantasy of marriage
was sewn together with ancestral threads, fashioned
by parents who were first cousins, whose intimacies
embraced horror and hiding from horror in bunkers
and graves, who shared the same family names,
the same losses of names.

Doris Ferleger

It helped, too, that my brother had assured me
that marriage was not irreversible; it was also useful
that I tended toward splitting from parts of myself
I couldn't tolerate and believed that air-brushed strokes
erased anything ugly in me from the eyes of others.
I also believed songs would fulfill their promises:
There's a place for us, somewhere a place for us.
Hold my hand and we're halfway there, somewhere.
Or perhaps I was more hopeful because I had not
as yet seen a dead naked body, had not as yet gagged
on the smell of formaldehyde in the med school's
cadaver room wondering whether the dead man
before me on the wooden table had a wife, whether
he had talked to her about mundane or awful things.

I see only now how in my childhood house, war welded
the awful to the mundane so they would never come apart.
Taking a shower led to talk of Auschwitz showers
and the scent of chamomile tea led to the way
my mother's hair smelled in Majdanek where Nazis
still gave them something to make them feel clean.

In the room full of dead bodies, in my first year
of marriage, I tried hard not to stare at Monique's
bird-light frame, her voluptuous breasts standing
like two never sleeping sentries, her startled eyes
reminding me that her first boyfriend had done
himself in. The three of us, hovering over the dead,
leaden with the weight of formaldehyde and last requests,
hopes, secrets, and revelations they might have offered.
I'm not saying I would have listened to their offerings.
I'm not saying I would have been wise enough to ask
for their help with my startled loneliness, though

the fine face of my husband slept against my left
shoulder each night, and each morning a strangely pleasant ache
stayed inside my shoulder for hours.

I didn't know that I wanted to be wanted, to be told
I was wanted, let alone anything beyond those wantings.
I didn't even know how to make myself happy and
no one there knew me well enough to ask if I was
and my mother who called weekly was willing
to believe in the good parts I told her, and I was
always sure to omit the hardness of the mattress
that lay flat against the grey unshining sheet-linoleum
that curled and buckled under our feet, and to omit
the morning my husband did a great kindness
by removing *The Bell Jar* from my hands in hopes
that it was the cause of my all too quiet crying.

But it was more that everything felt fallen
out of my hands, and I couldn't remember anything
about God except that my parents had replaced Him
with America after escaping from the ruined continent
on which I found myself, replacing Plath with Lessing's
Summer before the Dark about a doctor's wife who loses
her sense of place but holds tight at the neck, the knot
of her red scarf tied over her wild and grieving hair,
not unlike the scarf I myself owned for the pitifully wet
aching wind. *Summer before the Dark*— where dream
and myth conspire with the black and red forces of
a woman's life, impersonal forces, outrageous forces
that risk everything as they shoot down triple-decker
highways like Ferraris in L.A. or along the avenues
of the underworld where no one ever dies.

3.

It would take thirty years for my beloved to fall
on bended knee, (*which knee*, he had asked
a week before, *is the right knee?*) When he asked
for my hand I wept so long he wasn't sure
I'd say yes. It was our thirtieth wedding anniversary
and he had taken me to my favorite restaurant with
fine white linens, one slim votive candle and thirty-
foot high ceilings made of mahogany, my favorite wood.
Thirty years for all our body parts to gather together
as witnesses to the kind of love that saves lives
and has the large eyes of gratefulness.
Thirty years of joining ranks to face the dangers
of even delicate conflict, so afraid we were of losing
heart or the exquisite ache of the other. Thirty years
of storming each others' impeccable walls,
defense lines, each time with sturdier skills.
Thirty years of crossing each other's hyper-vigilant
borders in order to enter each other's torn countries,
thirty years to draw together— spine, heart, spleen.
Thirty years to find out that it's just another face
of love that wounds without wanting, that opens
doors better left closed and closes doors yearning
to be opened. Thirty years to do nothing
for the other but risk the possibility of death
or complete aliveness.

Doris Ferleger

NOTES

Fictitious names are used as needed in these poems.

"Dark Horse": *Chmielnik* was my father's hometown that was liquidated by the Nazis. *Judenfrei* means *free of Jews* in German.

"Rhinoplasty and a Mitzvah": The Druze are an Arabic people who practice an offshoot of Islam and live in small villages in Israel. *Mitzvah* means *good deed* in Hebrew.

"Doors and Windows": The epigraph comes from: www.hadassah.org.il/English/Eng.MainNavBar/About/ Art+at+Hadassah/-38k. The original Chagall windows are in the Hadassah-Hebrew University Medical Center in Jerusalem.

"Tanta Hoyna": *Tanta* means *auntie* in Yiddish. *Fashtunkina* means *stinky* in Yiddish. *Mun* means *poppy seed* in Yiddish/German.

"Spell to Be Said upon Hearing the Pain of a Loved One" was inspired by Jane Hirshfield's spell poems in *Lives of the Heart*.

"If All Is God": Rabbi Isaac Luria, leading 16th century Jewish mystic and poet, advanced the Kabbalistic concept that *tsimsum*, God's *withdrawal of light*, was necessary to produce human longing for God. According to this doctrine, light and darkness are nested opposites intrinsic to life and the creation process, not a fault or problem of humanity.

Special Thanks

Many thanks to: Vermont College of Fine Arts for providing a writing environment of opulent intelligence; special thanks to Nancy Eimers, Bill Olsen, Claire Rossini, Betsy Sholl, David Wojahn, and Leslie Ullman, as well as the Bread Loaf Writers Conference for vital conversations of craft and critique of poems in this book; Bill Olsen for generous mentoring on the manuscript; Leslie Ullman for thoughtful editing; Renee Rossi, Fran Abbate, Elizabeth Austen, Kathleen Fagley, Norma Schulman, Lisken Van Pelt Dus for close reading and critique. Thanks to: Natalie Goldberg, Tony Hoagland, Lori Lefkowitz, Naomi Shihab Nye, Sharon Olds and Elie Wiesel for words of support; Ed Hirsch and the Krakow Poetry Seminar where this book found its roots in Polish Poetry; Jason Shulman and IKH community for courage for the journey. Thanks to M. Scott Douglass for belief in this book.

For ongoing support, thanks to: Shelley Kiernan, Marsha Kroll, Mary Richardson Miller, Hayden Saunier, Janice Stridick, Susan Windle and her Philadelphia Writing Circle, Chris Bursk and the Bucks County poetry community, Joanne Leva and the Montgomery County Poetry Community. Special thanks to Polly Young Eisendrath for unwavering support over the years. Great gratitude goes to my family for abiding love, especially to my dearest Steven, who has listened and listened to my work and to my heart over so many years.